A Beginner's Guide to The Path of Shaivism:

"Embrace inner peace & spiritual transformation"

Chitvvan Waraich

urate
quratebooks.com

A BEGINNER'S GUIDE TO PATH OF SHAIVISM:

"Embrace Inner Peace & Spiritual Transformation
Chitvvan Waraich

Published in 2024

© Published by

Qurate Books Pvt. Ltd.
Goa 403523, India
www.quratebooks.com
Tel: 1800-210-6527, Email: info@quratebooks.com

ISBN: 978-93-58984-65-1

Acknowledgments

I extend my deepest gratitude to Lord Shiva, the supreme consciousness and the guiding light of my spiritual journey. It is through his divine grace and the profound teachings of Shaivism that I have been able to explore and share the depth of this sacred tradition. Lord Shiva's presence has been a constant source of inspiration and strength, illuminating my path and deepening my connection to the divine.

To all those who walk the path of Shaivism, past and present, your wisdom and dedication have been a torch for seekers like myself. I am deeply grateful for the guidance and support provided by the Shaiva community, whose insights and practices have enriched this book.

May this book serve as a humble offering, and may it inspire and guide others on their spiritual journey, just as Lord Shiva's teachings have guided me. Thank you for joining me in this exploration of the divine and the spiritual path of Shaivism.

"Om Tatpurushaya Vidmahe, Mahadevaya Dhimahi, Tanno Rudra Prachodayat."

Shiv Gayatri Mantra

"Har Har Mahadev "

Contents

Background

Understanding Shaivism: A Journey into the Ancient Path

Shaivism, one of the most profound and ancient traditions within Hinduism, centers on the worship of Lord Shiva. This spiritual path delves deep into the nature of existence, the divine, and the self, offering seekers a transformative journey toward self-realization and inner peace. This book serves as a guide for those who are new to Shaivism or seeking to deepen their understanding of this rich and intricate tradition.

Historical Roots and Evolution

The origins of Shaivism trace back to the pre-Vedic period, before the formalization of Hindu scriptures. It emerged from a blend of ancient spiritual practices and evolving philosophical ideas, which over time became a structured tradition with its own doctrines and rituals. Central to Shaivism is the belief in Shiva as the supreme consciousness that pervades all existence. Shiva's dual nature both the destroyer and the creator reflect the cyclical nature of the universe and life itself.

The tradition evolved through various schools of thought, each contributing to its depth and diversity. Notable among these are Kashmir Shaivism, which emphasizes the non-dual nature of reality, and Shaiva Siddhanta, which combines devotion with ritual practices to achieve spiritual goals. This book will explore these schools in detail, providing a comprehensive overview of their teachings and practices.

Core Philosophies & Practices

Shaivism teaches that the ultimate reality is Shiva, and that understanding this divine essence is key to achieving liberation (Moksha). The tradition integrates several core principles:

Non-Dualism (Advaita): Shaivism asserts that there is no separation between the divine and the material world. Everything is a manifestation of Shiva's consciousness.

Shakti (Divine Energy): Shakti represents the dynamic energy of the divine feminine, complementing Shiva's static consciousness. Together, they sustain the universe and guide spiritual practices.

Self-Realization: The path to spiritual enlightenment involves recognizing that one's true self (Atman) is one with Shiva. This realization is achieved through meditation, devotion, and self-inquiry.

Modern Relevance and Benefits

In today's fast-paced world, Shaivism offers valuable insights and practices for personal growth and spiritual development. Its emphasis on self-realization and inner peace provides a counterbalance to external chaos, helping individuals cultivate a deeper sense of purpose and fulfillment. Shaivism's holistic approach integrates mental, physical, and spiritual well-being, making it highly relevant for contemporary seekers.

Structure of the Book

This book is designed to guide you through the essential aspects of Shaivism in a clear and accessible manner. Each chapter will build on foundational concepts, exploring:

Historical Background: Detailed insights into the origins and evolution of Shaivism.

Core Teachings: Explanation of key philosophies and practices.

Practical Guidance: Step-by-step instructions for incorporating Shaivism into daily life.

Meditations and Practices: Techniques for spiritual growth and self-discovery.

As you embark on this journey, you will uncover the wisdom of Shaivism and learn how to apply its teachings to enhance your spiritual path. Whether you are a newcomer or someone seeking to deepen your practice, this book will provide you with the tools and understanding necessary to navigate and embrace the profound teachings of Shaivism.

Preface

Welcome to a journey through one of the most profound and ancient spiritual traditions: Shaivism. This book is designed for those who are curious about the path of Shaiva spirituality, whether you are just beginning your exploration or seeking to deepen your existing understanding.

As a devotee of Lord Shiva and a seeker of spiritual truth, I have been profoundly influenced by the teachings and practices of Shaivism. This tradition, with its deep roots in ancient wisdom, has not only enriched my life but has also provided a framework for spiritual growth and inner transformation. It is with great reverence and a deep sense of connection that I present this guide to Kashmir Shaivism—a path that has the power to illuminate your journey towards self-realization and divine understanding.

Shaivism is an ancient philosophical tradition centered on the worship of Shiva, one of the principal deities of Hinduism. Shiva is often depicted as the eternal yogi, embodying both the creative and destructive forces of the universe. His essence is both the source of all creation and the ultimate reality beyond creation. Shaivism explores this dual aspect of Shiva, offering a path that is both profound and transformative.

Why Follow Shaivism?

Shaivism provides a direct and intimate connection with the divine through practices such as meditation, mantra chanting, and rituals. This connection helps you experience the divine presence in your everyday life, fostering a deep sense of spiritual fulfillment.

At its core, Shaivism teaches that the ultimate goal of life is to realize that our true self (Atman) is one with Shiva, the supreme consciousness. This realization leads to liberation (Moksha) from the cycle of birth and rebirth and brings a profound sense of inner peace and freedom.

Shaivism also emphasizes the integration of mind and spirit, teaching practices that harmonize the physical, mental, and spiritual aspects of life. This holistic approach helps you achieve balance and well-being on all levels.

This book aims to make these profound concepts accessible and actionable, guiding you step by step on your spiritual journey. May it inspire and support you as you explore the transformative path of Shaivism, unlocking the wisdom and grace that lie within.

Short introduction to the book?

Hello and welcome to "A Beginner's Guide to Shaivism: Embracing Inner Peace & Spiritual Transformation

I'm honored to share this journey with you. My name is Chitvvan Waraich and I've been deeply connected to Lord Shiva since childhood. From a young age, I felt an inexplicable bond with Shiva's divine presence, so has my family had a deep connection and reverence for Mahadev including my grandparents and parents.

As I grew older, this connection evolved into a profound spiritual path. The teachings of Shaivism have not only shaped my understanding of the world but also brought me immense peace and clarity. It is this transformative experience that inspires me to write this book.

In these pages, I aim to offer you a clear and accessible introduction to Shaivism. My goal is to make the profound wisdom of this ancient practice approachable for anyone interested in exploring their own spiritual journey. Through simple explanations, practical exercises, and personal insights, I hope to help you connect with the divine essence of Lord Shiva and experience the inner peace that comes from walking this path.

Thank you for allowing me to be a part of your spiritual exploration. May you find inspiration, serenity, and a deeper connection to yourself and the divine.

Chapter 1

The Essence of Shaivism

Shaivism is a profound spiritual tradition that centers around the worship of Lord Shiva, one of the principal deities in Hinduism. At its core, Shaivism teaches that the divine essence, represented by Shiva, pervades all existence and that realizing this divine nature within ourselves leads to ultimate peace and fulfillment.

In this chapter, we'll explore the fundamental principles of Shaivism, its historical background, and key teachings that form the foundation of this spiritual path.

"The Divine Nature of Shiva"

At the heart of Shaivism is the concept of Shiva as the Supreme Being. Shiva is not just a god but the ultimate reality that underlies all creation. This divine essence, known as Shiva, is both the source and the ultimate goal of all existence.

The Absolute Reality, Shiva represents the absolute, unchanging reality beyond the physical world. This reality is eternal, infinite, and beyond human comprehension.

Shiva is often depicted as Nataraja, the cosmic dancer who performs the dance of creation, preservation, and destruction. This dance symbolizes the dynamic and ever-changing nature of the universe.

In Shaivism, the essence of Shiva is present within each of us, by recognizing this divine presence within ourselves, we can experience a deep connection with the divine.

Shaivism has a rich and ancient history that spans thousands of years. Its teachings have evolved over time, influenced by various philosophical and cultural developments.

Origins of Shaivism:

The origins of Shaivism can be traced back to the early Vedic texts and the Indus Valley Civilization. The worship of Shiva, in various forms, was an integral part of early Indian spirituality. Over the centuries, Shaivism absorbed influences from various philosophical schools and regional traditions. It became a major spiritual path with its own set of scriptures, rituals, and practices.

The Shiva Sutras: These texts provide insights into the nature of reality and the path to self-realization.

The Tantras: Tantric texts elaborate on the rituals, meditation practices, and philosophical teachings of Shaivism.

Shaivism offers a comprehensive framework for understanding the nature of reality and the self. Its teachings emphasize the importance of self-realization and direct experience of the divine.

The Concept of Atman

In Shaivism, the self (Atman) is seen as identical with Shiva. This means that our true nature is divine and infinite, beyond the limitations of the physical body and mind.

The goal of spiritual practice in Shaivism is to realize this divine nature and experience unity with the absolute reality.

Meditation is a key practice in Shaivism, used to quiet the mind and connect with the divine essence within.

Bhakti, or devotion, plays a significant role in Shaivism. It involves expressing love and reverence for Shiva, which helps in deepening the spiritual connection.

Why Follow Shaivism?

Following Shaivism offers numerous benefits for spiritual growth and personal development. By embracing its teachings, you can achieve a profound sense of inner peace and fulfillment.

Benefits of Shaivism are as follows :

1. **Inner Peace:** The practice of Shaivism helps calm the mind and reduces stress, leading to a deeper sense of inner tranquility.

2. **Self-Discovery:** Through its teachings and practices, Shaivism guides you in discovering your true self and realizing your divine nature.

3. **Spiritual Growth:** The path of Shaivism supports personal transformation and spiritual growth, helping you align with your highest potential.

As we move forward in this book, we will delve deeper into the practices and principles of Shaivism, offering practical guidance for integrating these teachings into your daily life. The goal is to make the spiritual journey accessible and meaningful, helping you connect with the divine essence within and experience the profound benefits of Shaivism.

Chapter 2

The History and Key Concepts of Shaivism

Shaivism, one of the major traditions within Hinduism, has a deep and fascinating history. To fully appreciate its teachings and practices, it's important to understand its evolution over time. This chapter will guide you through the historical development of Shaivism and introduce you to some of its key concepts.

Shaivism's roots can be traced back to ancient times, with its origins intertwined with the early spiritual practices of the Indus Valley Civilization.

Archaeological findings from this period, including seals and artifacts, suggest the worship of deities that resemble aspects of Shiva, such as the horned deity seen in the seals.

In the Vedic period the figure of Rudra, a storm and hunt god, began to merge with the concept of Shiva. Rudra was depicted as a fierce deity, and over time, his characteristics were incorporated into the larger figure of Shiva. This period laid the groundwork for many Shaiva practices and beliefs.

By the time of the classical texts, Shaivism had become a well-established tradition with its own set of scriptures and practices. The development of the Shaiva Siddhanta, a key philosophical system within Shaivism, occurred during this period. Shaiva Siddhanta emphasized the worship of Shiva as the ultimate reality and detailed complex rituals and cosmology.

The Tantric Tradition

In the early medieval period, the Tantric tradition emerged within Shaivism. The Tantras introduced a more esoteric approach to spiritual practice, focusing on rituals, meditation, and mystical experiences. The famous texts of the Tantric tradition include the Kularnava Tantra and the Rudra Yamala Tantra.

Key Concepts of Shaivism

The Nature of Shiva

Shiva is viewed as the Supreme Being in Shaivism, encompassing both creation and destruction. He represents the ultimate reality, known as Brahman, and is both immanent and transcendent.

The Cosmic Dancer (Nataraja): Shiva's dance symbolizes the cosmic cycles of creation, preservation, and destruction. This dance represents the dynamic nature of the universe.

The Yogi: Shiva is often depicted in deep meditation, highlighting his role as the ultimate yogi and ascetic.

The Concept of Atman

In Shaivism, Atman refers to the true self, which is considered to be divine and identical with Shiva. Understanding and realizing the true self is central to Shaiva practice.

Getting Started with Shaivism

As you embark on your journey with Shaivism, having a foundation in its history and key concepts will provide valuable insights and context. In the following chapters, we will delve into practical aspects of Shaiva practice, including meditation, devotion, and integrating Shaiva principles into daily life.

Chapter 3

Sacred Rituals and Practices

Understanding Rituals in Shaivism

Rituals are an important part of Shaivism. They help connect us with the divine, honor Shiva, and enhance our spiritual growth. This chapter will introduce you to the key rituals and practices in Shaivism, making it easy for you to start incorporating them into your daily life.

Daily Rituals

1. Morning Prayers and Offerings

Starting your day with morning prayers and offerings is a way to set a positive tone for the day and align yourself with divine energies.

Simple Morning Ritual: Begin your day with a few minutes of silence. Light a diya (oil lamp) and offer it to Shiva, while saying a few words of gratitude and seeking blessings. This can be done at a small altar or designated space at home.

Offering Water: Offering water to a small Shiva lingam (symbol of Shiva) is a common practice. It symbolizes purity and respect. Simply pour water gently over the lingam while reciting a short prayer or mantra.

2. Meditation Practices

Meditation helps calm the mind and connect with the divine essence within you.

Basic Meditation: Find a quiet spot and sit comfortably. Close your eyes and focus on your breath. Gradually, shift your attention to visualizing Shiva in your mind. Imagine his presence and let his image fill you with peace.

Guided Meditation: You can also use guided meditation recordings that focus on Shiva. These usually include soothing music and instructions to help you visualize and connect with divine energies.

Special Rituals

3. Puja (Worship) Ceremonies

Puja is a more elaborate ritual that involves offerings and prayers to honor Shiva.

Setting Up for Puja: Prepare a clean space for the puja. Place an image or a small Shiva lingam on a clean cloth. Gather items like flowers, incense sticks, a bell, and a diya.

Performing the Puja: Light the incense and diya, offer flowers to Shiva while reciting a prayer or mantra. Ring the bell gently as a sign of reverence. Conclude the puja by offering a small piece of food (prasad) and seeking blessings.

Meditation Retreats

Attending meditation retreats or workshops can deepen your practice and understanding of Shaivism.

Finding a Retreat: Look for local or online retreats that focus on Shaiva practices. These retreats often include meditation sessions, teachings on Shaiva philosophy, and communal worship.

Participating in Retreats: During the retreat, engage fully in the activities. Participate in group meditations, listen to teachings, and connect with others on the spiritual path.

Creating a Sacred Space

Having a dedicated space for your spiritual practices can make it easier to maintain consistency and focus.

Choosing a Location: Find a quiet and clean spot in your home where you can perform your rituals and meditations. This could be a corner of a room or a small room dedicated to your practice.

Setting Up the Space: Place a small altar with images or symbols of Shiva. Add items like candles, incense holders, and a small mat or cushion for sitting. Keep the space tidy and adorned with meaningful objects.

Incorporating Rituals into Daily Life

Integrating these rituals into your daily routine can enhance your spiritual growth and deepen your connection with Shiva.

Consistency: Try to perform morning prayers and meditation regularly. Consistency helps in building a strong spiritual practice.

Adaptation: Feel free to adapt the rituals to suit your personal preferences and schedule. The key is to maintain a sense of devotion and connection.

Benefits of Rituals

Performing these rituals and practices can lead to several benefits:

1. **Spiritual Growth:** Regular practice helps you connect with divine energies and enhances your spiritual awareness.

2. **Mental Calmness:** Rituals and meditation bring peace and reduce stress, contributing to overall mental well-being.

3. **Inner Fulfillment:** Engaging in rituals creates a sense of purpose and fulfillment, enriching your spiritual journey.

By incorporating these sacred rituals and practices into your life, you can deepen your connection with Shiva and support your spiritual growth. These practices are not just about performing rituals; they are about creating a meaningful connection with the divine and nurturing your inner self.

Chapter 4

The Role of Ayurveda and a Satvic Diet in Practicing Shaivism

Ayurveda, the ancient system of medicine and wellness, and the Satvic diet, which is rooted in purity and balance, play significant roles in the practice of Shaivism. For a Shaivite—one who follows the spiritual path dedicated to Lord Shiva—these elements are not merely about physical health but are deeply intertwined with spiritual growth and the practice of devotion.

Ayurveda in Shaivism

1. **Harmonizing Body and Mind:** Ayurveda focuses on maintaining balance in the body and mind through a holistic approach to health. For Shaivites, this balance is crucial for spiritual practices such as meditation, mantra chanting, and rituals, as it ensures that the body is in its optimal state to support spiritual endeavors.

2. **Cleansing and Purification:** Ayurvedic practices such as Panchakarma (detoxification treatments) are essential for

purifying the body of toxins, which can otherwise impede spiritual progress. A clean and pure body is believed to be a better vessel for spiritual energy, allowing one to connect more deeply with Lord Shiva.

3. **Mental Clarity and Focus:** Ayurveda emphasizes the importance of mental clarity, which is achieved through the right diet, herbs, and lifestyle practices. Mental clarity is vital in Shaivism, where deep meditation and focus are needed to connect with the divine and to understand the deeper truths of existence.

The Satvic Diet in Shaivism

1. **Purity of Diet, Purity of Mind:** The Satvic diet is a pure, clean, and energy-enhancing diet that consists of fresh fruits, vegetables, nuts, seeds, whole grains, and dairy in moderation. For Shaivites, consuming Satvic foods is believed to lead to a calm and peaceful mind, which is essential for meditation and spiritual practices.

2. **Enhancing Prana (Life Force):** Satvic foods are rich in prana, the life force that sustains all living beings. By consuming these foods, Shaivites believe they can increase their own prana, which in turn enhances their spiritual energy and capacity to perform spiritual practices such as yoga and chanting.

3. **Non-violence and Compassion:** The Satvic diet is rooted in the principle of ahimsa (non-violence). For a Shaivite, adhering to this diet is a way to practice compassion and non-violence, both of which are important tenets of Shaivism. This aligns with the spiritual goal of developing a loving and compassionate heart, akin to Lord Shiva's own nature.

4. **Supporting Meditation and Spiritual Practices:** Satvic foods are light and easy to digest, which helps in maintaining a balanced and calm state of mind. This is

particularly important for meditation, a central practice in Shaivism, where a peaceful and clear mind is necessary to reach deeper states of consciousness and connect with Shiva.

In the practice of Shaivism, Ayurveda and the Satvic diet serve as essential tools for maintaining the physical, mental, and spiritual purity needed to progress on the path of devotion. By following Ayurvedic principles and consuming a Satvic diet, a Shaivite can align their body, mind, and spirit with the divine energy of Lord Shiva, thus enhancing their spiritual journey and deepening their connection with the Supreme.

Chapter 5

Understanding the Shiv Puran

What is the Shiv Puran?

The Shiv Puran is one of the eighteen Mahapuranas, a genre of ancient Indian scriptures that serve as a major source of Hindu mythology. Dedicated primarily to Lord Shiva, this Puranic text is revered by Shaivites, devotees of Shiv, and provides a comprehensive overview of Shiva's role in the universe, his stories, teachings, and the principles of Shaivism.

Structure and Content

The Shiv Puran is composed of several sections, or Samhitas, each containing different types of narratives, hymns, and rituals associated with Shiva. The key elements covered in the Shiv Puran include:

Creation and Destruction: The Shiv Puran delves into the cyclical nature of the universe, where Shiva plays a crucial role in both creation and destruction. It describes how Shiva, as the cosmic dancer Nataraja, performs the dance of creation, preservation, and destruction, symbolizing the endless cycle of life.

Stories of Shiva: The text is filled with captivating stories about Lord Shiva, his consort Parvati, their children Ganesha and Kartikeya, and other divine beings. These stories are not only entertaining but also provide moral lessons and deeper spiritual insights.

Worship and Rituals: Detailed instructions on various forms of Shiva worship, including the significance of the Shivling (a symbolic representation of Shiva), are provided. The Shiv Puran outlines how devotees can perform rituals to gain Shiva's blessings and achieve spiritual growth.

Philosophy and Teachings: The text explores the philosophical aspects of Shaivism, emphasizing the importance of devotion, meditation, and ethical living. It teaches that true liberation (moksha) can be attained through sincere devotion to Shiva and understanding the oneness of the soul with the divine.

Why is the Shiv Puran Important?

For Shaivites, the Shiv Puran is a spiritual guide that offers a pathway to connect with the divine. It helps devotees understand the nature of Shiva, his cosmic roles, and how they can incorporate his teachings into their daily lives. The text also reinforces the concept of bhakti (devotion) and the importance of leading a righteous life.

The Shiv Puran is much more than just a collection of stories; it is a profound scripture that guides believers on their spiritual journey. By reading and understanding the Shiv Puran, one can gain deeper insights into the mysteries of life, the nature of the universe, and the eternal connection between the soul and the divine.

The Relevance of Shiv Puran in Modern Life:

The Shiv Puran is an ancient text, yet its teachings and stories hold timeless relevance, especially in today's fast-paced and often chaotic world. By delving into the Shiv Puran, individuals can find guidance, peace, and spiritual growth, making it a valuable resource for modern life.

1. **Finding Inner Peace and Balance:** In the Shiv Puran, Lord Shiva is often depicted as a figure of immense calm, even in the face of chaos. This imagery serves as a powerful reminder for people today who are overwhelmed by stress and the demands of modern life. Reading the Shiv Puran can help individuals cultivate a sense of inner peace, teaching them the importance of balance and stillness, much like Shiva's meditative state on Mount Kailash.

2. **Guidance on Ethical Living:** The stories and teachings in the Shiv Puran emphasize values like truth, integrity, devotion, and compassion. In a world where moral dilemmas and ethical challenges are common, the Shiv Puran offers timeless wisdom that can guide individuals in making decisions that align with these values, leading to a more fulfilling and righteous life.

3. **Strengthening Devotion and Spiritual Practice:** For those on a spiritual path, the Shiv Puran deepens their understanding of devotion (bhakti) and the practices that connect them with the divine. By engaging with this text, individuals can enhance their spiritual practices, such as meditation and mantra chanting, fostering a closer connection to Shiva and cultivating spiritual growth.

4. **Coping with Change and Transformation:** One of the central themes in the Shiv Puran is Shiva's role in the cycle of creation, preservation, and destruction. This concept can help individuals in modern life understand and accept the inevitability of change and transformation.

Whether facing personal or professional upheavals, the teachings of Shiva provide a framework for embracing change as a natural and necessary part of life.

Benefits of Reading the Shiv Puran and Performing Shiv Puran Katha Puja:

1. **Spiritual Upliftment:** Reading the Shiv Puran or participating in a Shiv Puran Katha (a ceremonial recitation and explanation of the text) elevates one's spiritual consciousness. It is believed that engaging with this sacred text brings one closer to the divine and enhances spiritual understanding.

2. **Mental Clarity and Focus:** The meditative aspects of the Shiv Puran and the calming effect of the stories can help improve mental clarity and focus. Regular reading or listening to the Shiv Puran can be a form of meditation, helping individuals clear their minds and concentrate better on their daily tasks.

3. **Positive Energy and Protection:** The Shiv Puran is said to generate positive energy and protect those who read it or listen to it with devotion. It is believed that the vibrations created by reciting or hearing the mantras and stories invoke Shiva's blessings, which can shield one from negative influences and attract positive outcomes.

4. **Community and Shared Devotion:** Participating in a Shiv Puran Katha is often a communal activity that brings people together in shared devotion. This fosters a sense of community, connection, and collective spiritual growth, which can be particularly beneficial in today's increasingly isolated and individualistic society.

5. **Healing and Purification:** Both the mind and body can benefit from the healing aspects of engaging with the Shiv Puran. The rituals and mantras associated with its reading and the Katha Puja are believed to purify one's

karma, heal past wounds, and bring about physical and emotional well-being.

The Shiv Puran is not just a collection of ancient stories; it is a living guide that can help individuals navigate the complexities of modern life with wisdom, peace, and spiritual depth. Whether through personal reading or participating in a Shiv Puran Katha Puja, the teachings of Shiva can provide profound benefits, helping individuals live more balanced, ethical, and spiritually connected lives.

Chapter 6

The Spiritual Symbolism in Shaivism

Shaivism, is rich with symbols that hold deep spiritual meaning. These symbols are not just artistic representations but are imbued with profound philosophical and spiritual concepts.

For beginners on the Shaiva path, understanding these symbols can greatly enhance their spiritual journey. In this chapter, we will explore some of the key symbols in Shaivism, their meanings, and how they are used in spiritual practices.

Symbols and Their Meanings

The Trishula (Trident):

The trishula, or trident, is one of Lord Shiva's most iconic symbols. This three-pronged weapon represents the three fundamental aspects of existence: creation, preservation, and destruction. It symbolizes Shiva's control over the three worlds (physical, mental, and spiritual) and his ability to transcend time, represented by the past, present, and future.

For a spiritual practitioner, the trishula also serves as a reminder to balance and harmonize these forces within oneself. It encourages the practitioner to maintain a state of equilibrium, embracing all aspects of life without attachment.

The Damru (Drum):

The damru, a small two-headed drum, is often seen in Shiva's hand. This instrument holds deep symbolic significance in Shaivism. The damru represents the cosmic sound, or Nada, which is the source of creation. It is believed that the rhythmic beats of the damru symbolize the cycle of creation and dissolution, echoing the rhythm of the universe.

The sound produced by the damru is also seen as the source of sacred mantras. When chanted, these mantras create vibrations that resonate with the energy of the universe, aligning the practitioner with the cosmic order.

The Third Eye:

Shiva's third eye, located in the center of his forehead, is a powerful symbol of spiritual awakening and wisdom. It represents the inner eye or the eye of insight, which sees beyond the material world and perceives the truth hidden behind illusions.

The third eye is also associated with the destruction of evil and ignorance. When Shiva opens his third eye, it is said to unleash a fire that burns away impurities and illusions, symbolizing the transformative power of divine wisdom.

For practitioners, the third eye signifies the importance of developing inner vision through meditation and spiritual practices, transcending the limitations of ordinary perception.

The Linga and Its Significance

One of the most revered symbols in Shaivism is the Shivling or Linga. The Shivling is not just an object of worship but a profound symbol of the formless, infinite nature of the divine.

The Linga: The word "Linga" means "sign" or "symbol." In Shaivism, the Shivling represents the formless and all-pervading nature of Lord Shiva. Unlike traditional idols that have a defined form, the Linga is an abstract representation, signifying the unmanifested aspect of the divine. It embodies the idea that the divine transcends form and can be experienced as pure consciousness.

The Yoni: Often, the Linga is depicted with a base called the Yoni, which represents Shakti, the divine feminine energy. The union of the Linga and Yoni symbolizes the inseparable nature of Shiva and Shakti, the masculine and feminine principles that together create and sustain the universe.

Worship of the Shivling: In Shaiva rituals, the Shivling is bathed with water, milk, and other offerings, symbolizing the continuous process of creation and the flow of divine grace. For devotees, worshipping the Shivling is a way to connect with the formless divine and experience the presence of Shiva in their lives.

Symbolism in Rituals

In Shaivism, rituals are rich with symbolic elements that deepen the spiritual experience. These symbols are not merely decorative but serve as tools to connect the practitioner with the divine.

Abhishekam (Ritual Bathing): During the abhishekam, the Shivling is bathed with water, milk, honey, and other substances. Each element used in the ritual has its own significance. For example, water represents purity and the flow of life, while milk symbolizes the nurturing aspect of the divine. This ritual act symbolizes the purification of the soul and the outpouring of devotion towards Shiva.

Lighting of Lamps: Lamps are lit during Shaiva rituals to symbolize the dispelling of darkness and ignorance by the light of divine wisdom. The flame of the lamp represents the presence of Shiva, who is the inner light that guides the soul towards liberation.

Offering of Bilva Leaves: The Bilva (or Bael) leaf is considered sacred in Shaivism and is commonly offered to the Shivling. The three leaves of the Bilva are said to represent the three eyes of Shiva, the three Gunas (qualities) of nature, or the three deities (Brahma, Vishnu, and Shiva) of the Hindu trinity. Offering Bilva leaves is a symbolic act of surrendering the self to Shiva, seeking his grace and blessings.

The symbols in Shaivism are powerful tools that guide practitioners on their spiritual journey. Each symbol, whether it is the trishula, damru, third eye, or the Shivling, carries deep philosophical and spiritual meaning, helping devotees connect with the divine on a deeper level. By understanding and meditating on these symbols, practitioners can enhance their spiritual practices and experience the profound presence of Lord Shiva in their lives.

Chapter 7

The Role of Mantras in Shaivism

Introduction to Mantras

Mantras hold a sacred place in Shaivism, acting as powerful tools for spiritual transformation and connection with the divine. In the Shaiva tradition, mantras are considered vibrational formulas that can influence the mind, body, and spirit. Each mantra is a unique sound or phrase imbued with spiritual energy, intended to align the practitioner's consciousness with the divine presence of Lord Shiva.

Mantras are not mere words but are seen as carriers of divine energy, capable of transforming the practitioner's inner and outer worlds. They are used to calm the mind, purify the heart, and deepen one's connection to the divine. The sound vibrations of the mantras resonate within the practitioner, creating a bridge between the individual and the cosmic consciousness.

Popular Shaiva Mantras

Om Namah Shivaya:

Meaning: "I bow to Lord Shiva."

Significance: This is one of the most popular and revered mantras in Shaivism. It is considered a panchakshara mantra, meaning it has five syllables (Na, Ma, Shi, Va, Ya), each representing an element of the universe—earth, water, fire, air, and ether. Chanting this mantra helps the practitioner connect deeply with the essence of Lord Shiva, invoking his blessings for spiritual growth and inner peace.

Mahamrityunjaya Mantra:

Meaning: "We Meditate on the Three-Eyed One (Lord Shiva) who permeates and nourishes all like a fragrance. May He liberate us from the bondage of worldly life and death, bestowing the nectar of immortality."

Significance: Also known as the "Death Conquering Mantra," this powerful mantra is believed to bestow health, longevity, and protection from untimely death. It is often chanted for healing purposes and to invoke Shiva's blessings during difficult times. The mantra is associated with Lord Shiva's three-eyed form, representing his ability to see beyond time and space.

Shiva Gayatri Mantra:

Meaning: "We meditate on the supreme Lord, the Three-Eyed One (Shiva), who embodies all virtues. May He enlighten our intellect and guide us on the righteous path."

Significance: The Shiva Gayatri Mantra is a prayer for enlightenment, wisdom, and spiritual awakening. It is a shorter form of prayer that can be used in daily sadhana to align the practitioner's intellect and consciousness with the divine wisdom of Lord Shiva.

Chanting Techniques

Proper chanting of mantras is essential to harness their full spiritual potential. The sound vibrations created by chanting resonate within the body and mind, producing a calming and purifying effect. Here are some techniques to consider:

Breathing Techniques:

Inhale deeply before each recitation to fill the lungs with air. This helps to produce a strong, clear sound when chanting the mantra.

Exhale slowly as you chant, allowing the sound to resonate fully. Controlled breathing enhances focus and allows for a more profound spiritual experience.

Mental Focus:

Concentrate on the meaning and intent of the mantra as you chant. Visualize the form of Lord Shiva or a symbol associated with him, such as the Shiva Linga or the sacred Mount Kailash.

Keep the mind free from distractions, focusing solely on the sound of the mantra and its spiritual significance. This mental focus helps to deepen the connection with the divine.

Vibration and Resonance:

Feel the vibrations of the mantra in your throat, chest, and heart as you chant. These vibrations are believed to purify the energy centers (chakras) in the body, promoting spiritual growth and well-being.

Chanting with awareness of these vibrations allows the practitioner to connect more deeply with the mantra's spiritual power.

Mantra Meditation

Mantra meditation is a practice that combines the repetition of a mantra with meditation to enhance spiritual awareness and connection. Here's how to practice mantra meditation:

1. **Choose a Mantra:** Select a mantra that resonates with you and your spiritual goals. For beginners, Om Namah Shivaya is an excellent choice due to its simplicity and profound significance.

2. **Find a Quiet Space:** Sit in a comfortable position in a quiet space where you won't be disturbed. Close your eyes and take a few deep breaths to center yourself.

3. **Start Chanting:** Begin chanting your chosen mantra slowly and steadily, either aloud or silently in your mind. Focus on the sound of the mantra and its meaning.

4. **Deepen the Meditation:** As you continue chanting, let your mind relax and focus solely on the mantra. If your mind wanders, gently bring it back to the mantra.

5. **End with Silence:** After chanting for a few minutes or longer, stop and sit in silence. Allow the energy of the mantra to settle within you, feeling its presence in your heart and mind.

6. **Regular Practice:** Make mantra meditation a regular part of your spiritual practice. Over time, you will find that the mantra becomes a powerful tool for inner peace, spiritual growth, and connection with Lord Shiva.

Mantras are potent spiritual tools in Shaivism, guiding practitioners on a path of inner transformation and connection with the divine. Whether through chanting or mantra meditation, these sacred sounds help to cultivate a deeper relationship with Lord Shiva, fostering spiritual growth, mental clarity, and a sense of peace. Regular practice of these mantras can bring profound changes to one's life, aligning the practitioner with the divine energy that pervades all existence.

Chapter 8

What is Sadhana in Shaivism?

Understanding Sadhana

In the Shaiva tradition, sadhana is more than just a practice; it is a disciplined path to spiritual growth and self-realization. The term "sadhana" comes from the Sanskrit root word "sadh," which means "to accomplish." In the context of Shaivism, sadhana refers to the systematic and disciplined spiritual practices that guide an individual towards the ultimate goal of union with Lord Shiva, the embodiment of divine consciousness.

Sadhana is the means by which a practitioner cultivates spiritual awareness, purifies the mind and body, and deepens their connection with the divine. It is a path that requires dedication, consistency, and devotion, leading the seeker to transcend the limitations of the physical world and realize their true nature as a reflection of the divine.

Types of Sadhana

Meditation (Dhyana):

Meditation is a fundamental practice in Shaivism, focusing the mind on the form of Lord Shiva or on a specific mantra. Through deep meditation, the practitioner quiets the mind, allowing the divine presence of Shiva to permeate their consciousness. Regular meditation helps in cultivating inner peace and spiritual insight.

Mantra Chanting (Japa):

Mantra chanting, or japa, involves the repetition of sacred sounds or phrases dedicated to Lord Shiva, such as "Om Namah Shivaya." This practice helps in aligning the practitioner's energy with the divine vibrations of the mantra, purifying the mind, and deepening spiritual awareness.

Yoga:

In Shaivism, yoga is not just physical exercise but a spiritual practice that integrates the body, mind, and soul. Practices like Hatha Yoga, Raja Yoga, and Kundalini Yoga are integral to Shaiva sadhana, aiding in the awakening of spiritual energy (Kundalini) and harmonizing it with the divine.

Rituals (Puja):

Rituals play a significant role in Shaiva sadhana. Daily puja, involving the offering of flowers, incense, and prayers to a Shiva Lingam or idol, helps in cultivating devotion and maintaining a direct connection with Lord Shiva. These rituals are expressions of love, reverence, and surrender to the divine.

Benefits of Sadhana

Regular practice of sadhana in Shaivism brings numerous benefits:

Spiritual Growth: Sadhana helps in awakening the spiritual potential within, leading to a deeper understanding of one's true nature and the universe.

Mental Clarity: Through meditation and mantra chanting, sadhana purifies the mind, removing negative thoughts and emotions, and fostering clarity, focus, and inner peace.

Connection with the Divine: Sadhana strengthens the bond between the practitioner and Lord Shiva, creating a sense of unity with the divine and enhancing spiritual experiences.

Physical Well-being: The practice of yoga as part of sadhana promotes physical health, flexibility, and vitality, supporting overall well-being.

Daily Sadhana Practices

For beginners, establishing a daily sadhana routine can be transformative. Here are some simple practices to incorporate into your day:

Morning Prayers: Start the day with a short prayer or chant dedicated to Lord Shiva, expressing gratitude and seeking guidance for the day ahead.

Meditation: Set aside at least 10-15 minutes for morning meditation. Focus on the breath or a Shiva mantra, allowing the mind to settle into a peaceful state.

Mantra Chanting: Chant a mantra like "Om Namah Shivaya" for a few minutes, either aloud or silently, to align your energy with divine vibrations.

Puja: Perform a simple puja at home, offering flowers, water, or incense to a Shiva Lingam or image. This ritual fosters devotion and sets a spiritual tone for the day.

Overcoming Challenges in Sadhana

Sadhana, though rewarding, is not without challenges. Common obstacles include a restless mind, lack of time, and wavering commitment. Here are some strategies to maintain consistency and devotion:

Set Realistic Goals: Begin with small, achievable goals in your sadhana practice, gradually increasing the duration and intensity as you progress.

Create a Sacred Space: Designate a quiet, clean space in your home for sadhana. Having a dedicated spot for practice helps in creating a conducive environment for spiritual work.

Consistency Over Intensity: It's more important to practice regularly than to engage in intense sessions sporadically. Even a few minutes of sincere practice each day can lead to significant spiritual growth.

Seek Guidance: If you encounter difficulties, seek guidance from a teacher or spiritual community. Having a support system can help you stay motivated and overcome challenges.

Advanced Sadhana Practices

For those looking to deepen their spiritual journey, advanced sadhana practices offer more profound experiences and insights:

Kundalini Yoga: This advanced form of yoga focuses on awakening the dormant spiritual energy (Kundalini) at the base of the spine and guiding it upwards through the chakras, leading to spiritual enlightenment.

Raja Yoga: Also known as the "Royal Path," Raja Yoga involves the practice of deep meditation and self-discipline to control the mind and emotions, ultimately leading to self-realization.

Tantra Sadhana: In Shaivism, certain Tantra practices involve the use of rituals, mantras, and meditation to explore and transcend the limitations of the physical world, connecting with the divine on a deeper level.

Sadhana in Shaivism is a disciplined path that leads to spiritual growth, mental clarity, and a deep connection with Lord Shiva. Whether through meditation, mantra chanting, yoga, or rituals, each practice within sadhana is a step towards realizing the divine presence within and around us. By embracing sadhana with sincerity and devotion, practitioners can experience profound transformation, aligning their lives with the eternal wisdom and grace of Lord Shiva.

Chapter 9

The Path of Bhakti

Devotion, or Bhakti, plays a vital role in Shaivism and spiritual practice. It involves a deep, heartfelt connection to the divine and enriches your spiritual journey. In this chapter, we will explore the concept of Bhakti, how it enhances your practice, and practical ways to express your devotion.

What is Bhakti?

Bhakti, in Shaivism and broader Hindu traditions, refers to a profound love and devotion towards the divine. It is the practice of expressing your reverence and surrender to God, in this case, Lord Shiva. Bhakti is not just about rituals but about forming a genuine, heartfelt relationship with the divine.

Why Devotion Matters?

Bhakti deepens your connection with Shiva, allowing you to experience his divine presence and guidance more intimately.

Devotion nurtures qualities like love, compassion, and humility. By focusing on the divine, you cultivate these virtues within yourself. Devotion complements meditation and mindfulness. It brings an emotional dimension to your practice, making your spiritual journey more fulfilling.

Expressing Devotion Through Prayer and Rituals

Daily Prayers: Start your day with a simple prayer to Shiva. This can be a traditional prayer or one you create from the heart. Offer gratitude for the divine guidance and ask for blessings for the day ahead.

Puja (Ritual Worship): Perform puja to honor Shiva. This involves offering flowers, incense, and light (aarti) to his image or symbol. The ritual can be as elaborate or simple as you prefer. It's the intention and devotion that matter most.

Mantra Chanting: Chanting mantras, such as "Om Namah Shivaya," helps focus your mind on Shiva and invoke his energies. Regular chanting can enhance your devotion and spiritual practice.

Building a Personal Relationship with Shiva

1. **Visualizations:** Imagine Shiva in your mind, visualizing his divine form, and focus on his attributes. This helps in creating a personal connection with him.

2. **Write a Letter:** Write a heartfelt letter to Shiva expressing your feelings, gratitude, and requests. This act of writing can be a powerful way to connect and communicate with the divine.

3. **Devotional Music:** Listen to or sing devotional songs dedicated to Shiva. Music has a unique way of reaching the heart and can deepen your sense of devotion.

4. **Building a Connection:** Developing a Deeper Relationship with the Divine

5. **Surrender and Trust:** True devotion involves surrendering your ego and trusting in Shiva's plan for you. Let go of your worries and surrender them to the divine. This act of trust enhances your connection with Shiva.

6. **Regular Practice:** Consistency in devotional practices helps build a stronger relationship with Shiva. Make devotion a regular part of your life, not just during special occasions or needs.

7. **Seek Guidance:** If you're new to devotion, seek guidance from experienced practitioners or spiritual teachers. Their insights can help you navigate your devotional journey.

Understanding Surrender

Surrender in devotion means offering yourself completely to Shiva. It's about letting go of control and trusting in the divine will. This surrender can be a transformative experience, leading to greater peace and spiritual growth.

Building Trust

Trust in the divine involves believing that Shiva's guidance and blessings are always with you, even when things seem challenging. Trust helps you remain steadfast in your devotion and continue on your spiritual path with confidence.

Embracing Devotion as a Path

Devotion is not just an act but a path. It involves integrating the principles of Bhakti into all aspects of your life. By embracing devotion wholeheartedly, you invite divine grace and transform your spiritual journey.

Stories of Devotees and Cultivating Bhakti in Daily Life

Throughout history, countless devotees of Lord Shiva have demonstrated unwavering faith and devotion, serving as an inspiration for others on the spiritual path. These stories highlight the power of Bhakti (devotion) and how it transforms lives. Here, we will explore a few such stories that illustrate the deep connection between the devotee and the divine.

Kannappa Nayanar:

Kannappa was a hunter who became one of the 63 Nayanars (devoted saints) in the Shaiva tradition. His devotion to Shiva was so pure and intense that it transcended conventional forms of worship. Kannappa would offer Shiva the best of his hunts, including meat and water from his mouth, as a sign of his love. One day, seeing blood oozing from one of the eyes of the Shivling, Kannappa, in his deep devotion, plucked out one of his own eyes and placed it on the Linga. When the second eye began to bleed, Kannappa was ready to sacrifice his other eye. Moved by his devotion, Lord Shiva appeared before him and blessed him with divine vision, restoring both his eyes.

Basava:

Basava, a 12th-century philosopher and poet, was a prominent devotee of Lord Shiva. He is the founder of the Lingayat sect and a reformer who advocated for equality and social justice. Basava's life was dedicated to spreading the teachings of Shiva and inspiring people to lead lives rooted in devotion, compassion, and humility. His vachanas (poetic verses) reflect his deep connection to Shiva and his belief in the power of Bhakti to overcome all obstacles.

Ravana:

Ravana, the king of Lanka and the antagonist in the Ramayana, was also a devout follower of Lord Shiva. Despite his eventual downfall due to his ego, Ravana's devotion to Shiva was unwavering. He is said to have composed the Shiv Tandav Stotra, a powerful hymn in praise of Shiva, while playing the veena made from his own entrails. This story underscores the idea that devotion to Shiva transcends conventional morality and can be found even in those who are otherwise seen as antagonistic.

Bhakti in Daily Life

Devotion, or Bhakti, is not just an abstract concept confined to temples or rituals; it is a way of life that can be woven into every aspect of our daily existence. Cultivating Bhakti in everyday activities can lead to spiritual growth and a deeper connection with the divine.

Morning Rituals:

Start your day with a simple prayer or mantra dedicated to Lord Shiva. Reciting "Om Namah Shivaya" or the Mahamrityunjaya Mantra can set a positive tone for the day and align your mind with spiritual goals. This practice helps to purify the mind and connect with Shiva's energy, invoking his blessings for the day ahead.

Mindful Actions:

Incorporate mindfulness into your daily tasks as an expression of devotion. Whether it's cooking, cleaning, or working, perform each action with full awareness and gratitude, dedicating it to Shiva. This transforms mundane activities into spiritual practices, fostering a sense of peace and purpose.

Offering Food:

Before eating, offer a portion of your food to Shiva. This simple act of offering, known as Naivedya, reminds us that everything we have is a blessing from the divine. It also cultivates humility and gratitude, key aspects of Bhakti.

Japa (Mantra Recitation):

Set aside a few minutes each day to practice Japa, the repetition of a mantra. This can be done silently, aloud, or mentally, and helps to focus the mind on Shiva, gradually deepening your devotion. Over time, Japa can bring about a profound inner transformation, fostering a sense of oneness with the divine.

Evening Reflection:

At the end of the day, take a few moments to reflect on your actions and thoughts. Offer any mistakes or challenges to Shiva, asking for his guidance and strength to do better tomorrow. This practice of self-reflection, known as Atma Vichara, is an essential part of spiritual growth and helps to keep the mind aligned with divine principles.

The stories of Shaiva devotees like Kannappa, Basava, and Ravana illustrate the transformative power of Bhakti and its ability to bring us closer to Lord Shiva. By incorporating simple devotional practices into our daily lives, we can cultivate a deep and enduring connection with the divine, leading to spiritual growth and inner peace. Whether through prayer, mindfulness, or mantra recitation, Bhakti in daily life offers a path to a more meaningful and spiritually fulfilling existence.

Chapter 10

The Role of Yoga in Shaivism

In the tradition of Shaivism, yoga is not just a physical practice but a profound spiritual journey that aligns the body, mind, and soul with the divine essence of Lord Shiva. The word "yoga" itself means "union," and in Shaivism, this union is the merging of the individual soul (Atman) with the universal consciousness (Shiva). Yoga is an essential path in Shaivism for attaining spiritual growth, self-realization, and ultimate liberation (moksha).

Types of Yoga in Shaivism

Shaivism encompasses several types of yoga, each with its unique practices and goals. These yogic paths offer different approaches for spiritual seekers to connect with Shiva:

Jnana Yoga (Path of Knowledge)

Practice: This path emphasizes the pursuit of spiritual knowledge and wisdom. It involves deep study of scriptures like the Shiv Puran and meditative contemplation to realize the non-dual nature of the self and Shiva.

How to Practice: Devotees can start by reading sacred texts, engaging in self-inquiry (asking "Who am I?"), and meditating on the teachings of Shiva to cultivate inner wisdom.

Bhakti Yoga (Path of Devotion)

Practice: Bhakti Yoga focuses on devotion and love for Lord Shiva. It involves practices like chanting mantras, performing rituals, and engaging in heartfelt prayers to cultivate a deep, personal relationship with Shiva.

How to Practice: Begin by dedicating time each day to chant Shiva's names (like "Om Namah Shivaya"), participate in puja (worship rituals), and meditate on Shiva's divine form with love and devotion.

Karma Yoga (Path of Selfless Action)

Practice: Karma Yoga in Shaivism is about performing one's duties and actions without attachment to the outcomes, dedicating all efforts to Shiva. It teaches the importance of selfless service and humility.

How to Practice: Engage in daily activities with a sense of duty, offering the fruits of your actions to Shiva. Volunteer in temples, help others, and perform acts of kindness without expecting anything in return.

Raja Yoga (Path of Meditation and Control)

Practice: Raja Yoga, also known as Ashtanga Yoga, focuses on mastering the mind and body through meditation, breath control (pranayama), and physical postures (asanas). It aims to achieve a deep state of meditation and inner peace.

How to Practice: Start with simple meditation techniques, such as focusing on the breath or chanting a mantra. Incorporate basic yoga postures to prepare the body for meditation, and gradually deepen your practice with breath control exercises.

Kriya Yoga (Path of Rituals and Inner Transformation)

Practice: Kriya Yoga involves specific techniques and rituals that purify the body and mind, leading to spiritual awakening. It combines aspects of mantra chanting, pranayama, and meditation.

How to Practice: Learn from a qualified teacher who can guide you in specific kriya techniques. Begin with simple rituals, like lighting a lamp for Shiva, and gradually incorporate advanced practices as you progress on your spiritual journey.

Yoga in Shaivism is more than just physical exercise; it is a holistic approach to achieving spiritual enlightenment. Each type of yoga offers a different path to connecting with Shiva, catering to the diverse needs and temperaments of spiritual seekers. Whether through knowledge, devotion, action, meditation, or rituals, yoga helps individuals transcend the limitations of the ego, realize their true nature, and merge with the divine essence of Shiva.

How to Begin Your Yoga Practice in Shaivism

For beginners, starting a yoga practice in Shaivism can be simple yet profound. Here are some steps to help you get started:

Morning Meditation: Begin your day with a short meditation, focusing on Shiva. You can chant "Om Namah Shivaya" silently or aloud, allowing the mantra to resonate within you.

Daily Devotion: Dedicate a small space in your home as a shrine for Shiva. Offer flowers, light a lamp, and spend a few moments in prayer each day.

Read Sacred Texts: Choose a few verses from the Shiv Puran or other Shaiva scriptures and reflect on their meaning. This will deepen your understanding and connection to Shiva.

Practice Yoga Asanas: Incorporate simple yoga postures into your daily routine to keep the body healthy and prepare it for deeper meditation.

Engage in Selfless Service: Look for opportunities to help others in your community, offering your actions to Shiva as an act of devotion.

Conclusion

Yoga in Shaivism is a transformative practice that guides individuals on the path of spiritual growth and self-realization. By integrating the principles of Jnana, Bhakti, Karma, Raja, and Kriya Yoga into daily life, devotees can cultivate a deep connection with Shiva and progress on their journey towards enlightenment. Whether you are a beginner or an advanced practitioner, the teachings of Shaivism provide a rich and varied approach to yoga that nurtures the body, mind, and soul.

Chapter 11

Understanding Kundalini Shakti, and Yoga in Shaivism

In Shaivism, Kundalini Shakti is considered the divine feminine energy residing at the base of the spine, coiled like a serpent. This powerful force is both the source of all spiritual energy and the key to spiritual awakening. Kundalini Shakti is often referred to as the "serpent power," and when awakened, it rises through the chakras (energy centers) along the spine, leading to profound spiritual experiences and enlightenment.

What is Kundalini Kripa?

Kundalini Kripa refers to the grace or blessings of the awakened Kundalini. In Shaivism, this grace is seen as essential for spiritual growth. Kundalini Kripa is not something that can be forced; it is a divine gift that awakens when the time is right. Through dedicated spiritual practice, devotion, and the guidance of a guru, one can prepare to receive this grace. Once Kundalini is awakened, the practitioner experiences a deep transformation, leading to higher states of consciousness and union with Shiva, the universal consciousness.

The Role of Yoga in Awakening Kundalini

Yoga, in the Shaiva tradition, plays a crucial role in preparing the body and mind for the awakening of Kundalini Shakti. Specific types of yoga, such as Kundalini Yoga, focus on activating this dormant energy through a combination of physical postures (asanas), breath control (pranayama), meditation, and chanting of mantras.

Asanas: Certain yoga postures help open and align the chakras, allowing Kundalini energy to flow freely through the body.

Pranayama: Breath control techniques, such as alternate nostril breathing, purify the energy channels (nadis) and enhance the flow of prana (life force), facilitating the rise of Kundalini.

Meditation: Deep meditation helps the practitioner focus their mind and energies on Shiva, enabling a smoother and more controlled awakening of Kundalini.

Mantras: Chanting specific mantras, like "Om Namah Shivaya," resonates with the vibration of Kundalini Shakti and aids in her ascent through the chakras.

Benefits of Kundalini Awakening in Shaivism

Awakening Kundalini Shakti has profound benefits for both the spiritual and physical well-being of the practitioner:

1. **Spiritual Growth**: The rise of Kundalini leads to higher states of consciousness, allowing the practitioner to experience oneness with Shiva and attain spiritual enlightenment (moksha).

2. **Mental Clarity:** As Kundalini moves through the chakras, it purifies the mind, removing negative thoughts and emotions, and bringing clarity, peace, and inner stillness.

3. **Physical Health:** The flow of Kundalini energy revitalizes the body, improves health, and can even heal physical ailments by balancing the body's energy system.

4. **Emotional Healing:** Kundalini helps release deep-seated emotional blockages, leading to emotional balance, increased compassion, and a greater capacity for love.

How to Safely Practice Kundalini Yoga?

Kundalini Yoga should be practiced with care, as the awakening of Kundalini is a powerful and transformative experience. Here are some tips for safe practice:

Seek Guidance: It is essential to learn Kundalini Yoga from an experienced teacher or guru who can guide you through the process safely.

Start Slowly: Begin with basic yoga postures, pranayama, and meditation techniques to prepare your body and mind for the more advanced practices of Kundalini Yoga.

Listen to Your Body: Pay attention to your body's responses. If you feel discomfort or intense emotions, take a break and consult your teacher.

Practice Regularly: Consistency is key to gradually awakening Kundalini. Regular practice helps to gently raise the energy without overwhelming the system.

Maintain Purity: A satvik (pure) lifestyle, including a balanced diet, clean living, and a positive mindset, supports the safe awakening of Kundalini.

Kundalini Shakti, Kundalini Kripa, and yoga are integral aspects of spiritual practice in Shaivism. The awakening of Kundalini is a powerful journey towards self-realization and union with Shiva. Through disciplined yoga practice, guided by the principles of Shaivism, practitioners can safely awaken this divine energy, experiencing its transformative benefits on the path to enlightenment.

Chapter 12

Getting Started on the Path

Starting a spiritual journey can be both exciting and challenging. This chapter will guide you on how to cultivate the right mindset, set spiritual goals, and establish daily practices that will help you stay focused and motivated on your path.

Beginner's Mindset

1. **Cultivating Openness and Receptivity:** To embark on your spiritual journey, it's crucial to approach it with an open mind and heart. This mindset will help you absorb new teachings and experiences without judgment.

2. **Be Curious:** Approach Shaivism with curiosity and a willingness to learn. It's okay to not know everything right away. Allow yourself to explore and discover at your own pace.

3. **Embrace New Experiences:** Be open to trying new practices, rituals, and teachings. Every experience,

whether it seems small or significant, contributes to your spiritual growth.

4. **Let Go of Preconceived Notions:** Try to release any preconceived ideas or expectations about spiritual practices. This openness will help you connect more deeply with the teachings of Shaivism.

5. **Maintaining a Receptive Attitude:** Being receptive means being willing to accept and integrate new ideas and experiences into your life.

6. **Practice Mindfulness:** Pay attention to your thoughts and feelings during your spiritual practices. Notice how they evolve over time and be open to change.

7. **Stay Present:** Focus on the present moment during your rituals and meditations. This will help you fully engage with your practices and gain more from them.

Setting Spiritual Goals

Setting goals helps provide direction and purpose for your spiritual journey. Here's how to set goals that are both realistic and meaningful:

1. **Identify Your Aspirations:** Think about what you hope to achieve through your spiritual practice. This could be a deeper connection with Shiva, inner peace, or personal growth.

2. **Set Specific Goals:** Break down your aspirations into specific, achievable goals. For example, you might set a goal to meditate for 10 minutes each morning or to perform a weekly puja.

3. **Create a Plan:** Develop a simple plan to reach your goals. Outline the steps you need to take and set a timeline for achieving them.

Ensure that your goals align with your overall spiritual aspirations and the teachings of Shaivism.

Reflect on Your Values: Consider how your goals reflect your values and beliefs. Make sure they resonate with the principles of Shaivism, such as devotion, self-awareness, and inner peace.

Adjust as Needed: Be flexible and willing to adjust your goals as you grow and learn more about yourself and Shaivism.

Daily Practices

1. **Simple Meditation Practices:** Starting your day with meditation can help set a positive tone and bring focus to your spiritual practices.

2. **Basic Meditation:** Find a quiet place where you can sit comfortably. Close your eyes and focus on your breath. As you breathe deeply, try to clear your mind and focus on the presence of Shiva.

3. **Visualization Meditation:** Visualize Shiva in your mind, imagining his presence and feeling his divine energy. This can help you connect with his essence and start your day with a sense of calm.

Basic Ritual Practices

Incorporating simple rituals into your daily routine can help you maintain a spiritual focus and honor Shiva.

Morning Offerings: Begin your day by lighting a diya (oil lamp) and offering it to Shiva. You can also offer flowers or water to a small Shiva lingam. This act of devotion helps center your mind and spirit.

Evening Reflection: At the end of the day, take a few moments to reflect on your experiences and express gratitude. Light a candle, say a short prayer, and offer thanks for the day's experiences.

Setting Intentions: Setting intentions helps focus your spiritual practices and aligns them with your personal goals.

Formulating Intentions: Before starting your daily practices, take a moment to set an intention. This could be a specific goal you want to achieve or a quality you wish to cultivate, such as patience or compassion.

Staying Focused: Throughout the day, remind yourself of your intention. Let it guide your actions and decisions, helping you stay aligned with your spiritual goals.

Tips for Maintaining Consistency

Create a Routine: Establish a daily routine that includes your meditation and ritual practices. Consistency helps build a strong foundation for your spiritual journey.

Be Patient: Spiritual growth takes time. Be patient with yourself and allow your practice to evolve naturally.

Stay Motivated: Keep track of your progress and celebrate small achievements. This will help you stay motivated and committed to your path.

By cultivating the right mindset, setting achievable goals, and incorporating daily practices into your life, you'll create a strong foundation for your spiritual journey.

Remember that every small step you take contributes to your growth and connection with Shiva.

Chapter 13

Meditations and Mindfulness in Shaivism

Meditation and mindfulness are central practices in Shaivism, providing a pathway to deepen your spiritual experience and connect more intimately with the divine. This chapter will guide you through the purpose and benefits of meditation, introduce various meditation techniques, and explore mindfulness practices that you can incorporate into your daily life.

Introduction to Meditation

Meditation in Shaivism is more than just a practice; it's a means of connecting with the divine and understanding the self on a deeper level. Here's why meditation is so significant:

Through meditation, you can establish a direct connection with Shiva, the supreme consciousness. This connection helps you experience divine presence and guidance in your life. Regular meditation helps calm the mind, reduce stress, and promote a sense of inner peace. It creates a space for tranquility amid life's chaos.

Meditation also facilitates self-discovery and realization. It allows you to explore your inner self and uncover your true nature as divine and connected to Shiva.

Different Types of Meditation Practices

Shaivism encompasses various meditation techniques, each offering unique benefits. Here are some common practices:

1. **Dhyan (Focused Meditation):** This involves concentrating on a specific object, such as a deity, a mantra, or your breath. Dhyan helps develop mental clarity and deepen your spiritual focus.

2. **Shiva Meditation:** In this practice, you visualize Shiva and focus on his attributes and qualities. This meditation helps you connect with Shiva's divine essence and absorb his energies.

3. **Mantra Meditation:** Chanting or silently repeating a mantra, such as "Om Namah Shivaya," helps you align your mind with divine vibrations and cultivate inner stillness.

4. **Guided Visualization:** Although not detailed here, guided visualization typically involves imagining specific scenarios or symbols related to Shiva, which helps in deepening the spiritual experience.

5. **Mindfulness Practices:** Mindfulness is the practice of being fully present and aware in each moment. Integrating mindfulness into your daily life can enhance your spiritual growth and overall well-being.

* Techniques for Integrating Mindfulness into Daily Life*

Mindful Breathing: Take a few moments throughout the day to focus on your breath. Pay attention to each inhale and exhale, helping you stay grounded and present.

Mindful Eating: When eating, focus on the flavors, textures, and sensations of your food. This practice encourages appreciation for the nourishment you receive and fosters a sense of gratitude.

Mindful Walking: As you walk, pay attention to the sensation of each step and the rhythm of your movement. This practice helps you connect with the present moment and enjoy the journey.

Maintaining Awareness : Maintaining awareness throughout your day supports spiritual practice and helps you remain centered.

Set Reminders: Use gentle reminders, such as alarms or notes, to pause and take a moment for mindfulness. This can be a simple practice like deep breathing or a brief reflection.

Practice Gratitude: Regularly express gratitude for the small and big things in life. This practice enhances your awareness of the positive aspects of your daily experiences.

Observe Without Judgment: When practicing mindfulness, observe your thoughts and feelings without judgment. This approach helps you understand your inner landscape and promotes self-compassion.

Incorporating Meditation and Mindfulness into Your Routine

1. **Create a Routine:** Establishing a routine for meditation and mindfulness helps make these practices a natural part of your life.

2. **Choose a Time:** Find a time that works best for you, whether it's in the morning, during lunch, or before bed. Consistency helps in developing a regular practice.

3. **Designate a Space:** Create a dedicated space for meditation and mindfulness. This can be a quiet corner in your home where you feel comfortable and undisturbed.

If you're new to meditation and mindfulness, start with short periods and gradually increase the time as you become more comfortable.

Begin with 5-10 Minutes: Start with a few minutes of meditation or mindfulness each day. As you grow accustomed to the practice, you can extend the duration.

Be Patient: Progress in meditation and mindfulness takes time. Be patient with yourself and recognize that each moment of practice contributes to your overall growth.

By understanding the significance of meditation and mindfulness in Shaivism and incorporating these practices into your daily routine, you'll deepen your spiritual connection and enhance your journey toward self-realization. Remember that meditation and mindfulness are tools for exploring your inner self and connecting with the divine presence of Shiva.

Chapter 14

Shaivism and the Path of Spiritual Growth

Shaivism, a profound and ancient tradition, offers a comprehensive path for spiritual growth and self-realization. Rooted in the worship of Lord Shiva, it provides a unique framework for understanding the nature of existence and one's place within it. This chapter explores how Shaivism guides individuals on their spiritual journey, highlighting the benefits and transformative effects of following this path.

The Path of Spiritual Growth in Shaivism:

Shaivism offers a structured approach to spiritual growth, integrating various practices and principles designed to elevate consciousness and foster self-realization.

At the core of Shaivism is the realization of one's true self (Atman) as identical with the supreme consciousness (Shiva). This self-awareness is achieved through meditation, contemplation, and self-inquiry.

Regular meditation is central to the Shaiva path. Techniques such as focusing on the inner self, visualizing divine forms, and chanting mantras help in aligning one's consciousness with the divine and transcending the ego.

Rituals and devotional practices in Shaivism, such as puja (worship) and abhishekam (ritual bathing of the deity), create a sacred space for spiritual connection and expression of devotion. These practices help cultivate a deeper sense of reverence and connection to the divine.

In Shaivism, the guidance of a realized guru (teacher) is considered essential for spiritual progress. The guru imparts wisdom, offers practical teachings, and helps the disciple navigate the path to self-realization.

Benefits of Following the Shaiva Path:

Embracing Shaivism offers numerous benefits that contribute to personal and spiritual development. These benefits extend to various aspects of life, fostering holistic well-being and inner peace.

Inner Peace and Stability: Through practices like meditation and devotion, individuals experience a profound sense of inner peace and stability. This tranquility helps manage stress and cultivates emotional resilience.

Enhanced Self-Awareness: The Shaiva path promotes deep self-awareness, allowing individuals to understand their true nature and align their actions with their higher purpose. This self-knowledge leads to greater fulfillment and authenticity.

Spiritual Liberation: The ultimate goal of Shaivism is to attain spiritual liberation (moksha), which signifies freedom from the cycle of birth and rebirth (samsara). By realizing one's divine nature, individuals transcend worldly limitations and merge with the eternal consciousness.

Harmonious Living: Shaivism encourages living in harmony with oneself and the environment. Principles such as non-violence (ahimsa), truthfulness (satya), and compassion (karuna) guide ethical conduct and foster positive relationships.

Personal Transformation: The practices and teachings of Shaivism facilitate personal transformation by helping individuals overcome ego-based limitations, develop virtues, and embrace their higher potential.

Practical Steps for Incorporating Shaivism into Your Life:

To integrate Shaivism into your daily life and spiritual practice, consider the following steps:

Daily Meditation: Establish a regular meditation practice focusing on inner silence and connection with the divine. Use mantras and visualizations to deepen your practice.

Rituals and Worship: Participate in or create personal rituals that resonate with you, such as lighting a lamp, offering flowers, or reciting sacred texts. These acts of devotion help cultivate a spiritual atmosphere.

Study and Reflection: Engage in the study of Shaiva texts and teachings. Reflect on their meanings and how they apply to your life.

Seek Guidance: If possible, connect with a knowledgeable guru or spiritual guide who can offer insights and support on your journey.

Practice Virtues: Integrate Shaiva principles into your daily interactions, striving to live with compassion, integrity, and respect for all beings.

Conclusion:

Shaivism offers a profound path for spiritual growth and self-realization. By understanding its principles and incorporating its practices into your life, you can embark on a journey of deep personal transformation and spiritual fulfillment. Through meditation, devotion, and the guidance of a guru, you can align yourself with the divine essence and experience the true nature of existence. Embrace the Shaiva path with dedication and openness, and allow it to guide you towards inner peace, wisdom, and liberation.

Chapter 15

Integrating Shaivism into Everyday Life

Integrating the principles of Shaivism into your daily routine can bring spiritual depth and balance to your life. This chapter will guide you on creating daily rituals, applying Shaiva principles to modern challenges, and setting up a sacred space in your home.

1. **Daily Rituals:** Creating and Maintaining Daily Spiritual Routines

2. **Morning Rituals:** Start your day with a brief spiritual routine. This can include a few minutes of meditation, a simple prayer to Lord Shiva, or light stretching to connect with your body and mind. The key is to set a positive tone for the day.

3. **Mindful Eating:** Bring mindfulness to your meals. Before eating, offer gratitude for the food and the nourishment it provides. Eating with awareness aligns your daily activities with spiritual principles.

4. **Evening Reflection:** End your day with reflection or journaling. Review the day's events and express gratitude for the experiences. This practice helps you stay connected with your spiritual goals and provides insights into your growth.

Simple Rituals to Enhance Daily Life

1. **Light a Candle:** Lighting a candle as part of your evening routine symbolizes the illumination of knowledge and the dispelling of darkness. It's a simple yet profound way to bring a sense of spirituality into your home.

2. **Offer Flowers:** Placing fresh flowers at a small altar or in a sacred corner of your home can be a beautiful way to honor the divine and remind yourself of the beauty and sanctity of life.

3. **Use Sacred Symbols:** Incorporate symbols of Shiva, such as the trident or the Om symbol, into your daily surroundings. These symbols can serve as reminders of your spiritual journey and the divine presence in your life.

Living the Teachings, applying Shaiva Principles to modern challenges

Embrace Non-Attachment: In the hustle and bustle of daily life, practicing non-attachment can help you remain balanced and focused. This principle encourages you to engage with life fully but without clinging to outcomes or possessions.

Cultivate Compassion: Shaivism teaches the importance of compassion towards all beings. Incorporate acts of kindness and understanding in your interactions with others, fostering a sense of unity and connection.

Practice Equanimity: Maintain a sense of calm and balance regardless of external circumstances. This principle helps you navigate challenges with grace and stability, reflecting the inner peace cultivated through spiritual practice.

How to Embody Spiritual Values in Everyday Interactions

Mindful Communication: Practice speaking with intention and kindness. Be mindful of how your words affect others and aim to communicate with empathy and respect.

Work with Integrity: Apply spiritual values in your professional life by working with honesty and dedication. Approach your work as a form of service and an opportunity to contribute positively to the world.

Foster Community: Build relationships with others who share your spiritual values. Engaging with a community of like-minded individuals can provide support, encouragement, and shared wisdom on your spiritual path.

Creating a Sacred Space: Setting Up a Personal Space for Meditation and Reflection

Choosing a Location: Select a quiet and comfortable area in your home where you can create a sacred space. It should be free from distractions and conducive to meditation and reflection.

Designing Your Space: Decorate your sacred space with items that inspire and uplift you. This may include images of Shiva, candles, incense, or sacred texts. The space should feel inviting and support your spiritual practices.

Maintaining the Space: Keep your sacred space clean and orderly. Regularly refresh the area with new flowers or incense to maintain a sense of sanctity and focus.

Tips for Maintaining a Spiritual Environment at Home

Create a Routine: Dedicate specific times each day for your spiritual practices in your sacred space. This helps establish a routine and reinforces your commitment to your spiritual journey.

Incorporate Spiritual Reminders: Place spiritual reminders or affirmations in visible areas of your home. These can serve as prompts to bring mindfulness and intention into your daily life.

Involve Family: If you live with others, involve them in creating and maintaining the sacred space. Share your practices and explain the significance, fostering a supportive and harmonious environment.

Chapter 16

Stories from the Shiv Puran Related to Shaivism

The Shiv Puran is one of the most revered texts in Shaivism, offering deep insights into the life and teachings of Lord Shiva. It is filled with stories that illustrate Shiva's power, compassion, wisdom, and his role as the ultimate destroyer and transformer. These stories not only tell about Shiva but also provide valuable lessons for devotees, helping them understand the principles of Shaivism and their application in everyday life. Here, we will explore ten significant stories from the Shiv Puran and their connection to Shaivism.

1. The Birth of Lord Shiva

The Shiv Puran narrates that Shiva is both unborn and eternal, embodying the ultimate reality, beyond creation and destruction. However, in one version, he is said to have manifested as a fiery pillar of light with no beginning or end, symbolizing his transcendence.

Shaiva Significance: This story illustrates Shiva as the supreme reality, emphasizing his role as the eternal and formless one, central to Shaivism.

2. The Story of Sati and Shiva

Sati, the daughter of Daksha, marries Shiva against her father's wishes. Daksha later insults Shiva during a grand yagna (sacrifice), leading Sati to immolate herself in protest. Enraged, Shiva unleashes his wrath, destroying Daksha's yagna and ultimately restoring order.

Shaiva Significance: This story highlights the themes of devotion, love, and the consequences of ego. It also shows Shiva's role as both the loving husband and the fierce destroyer of arrogance and disrespect towards the divine.

3. The Churning of the Ocean (Samudra Manthan)

During the churning of the ocean by the gods and demons to obtain Amrita (nectar of immortality), a deadly poison called Halahala emerges, threatening to destroy the universe. Shiva, in his infinite compassion, consumes the poison, holding it in his throat, which turns blue, earning him the name Neelkanth.

Shaiva Significance: This story underscores Shiva's role as the protector of the universe, willing to sacrifice himself for the greater good. It also symbolizes the idea of transforming poison (negativity) into something that can be controlled and contained, a key aspect of spiritual practice.

4. The Tale of Ganga's Descent

King Bhagiratha performs severe penance to bring the river Ganga down from the heavens to earth to purify the ashes of his ancestors. However, Ganga's descent threatens to flood the earth, so Shiva agrees to capture her in his matted hair, releasing her gently as streams.

Shaiva Significance: This story highlights Shiva's role as the compassionate deity who balances the cosmic forces, protecting the earth from devastation while granting boons to his devotees.

5. The Birth of Kartikeya

The demon Tarakasura receives a boon that only a son of Shiva could kill him. Shiva and Parvati's son, Kartikeya, is born to fulfill this prophecy and eventually defeats Tarakasura.

Shaiva Significance: This story emphasizes the concept of divine intervention through Shiva's lineage, showing how Shiva's progeny play a crucial role in maintaining cosmic order.

6. The Destruction of Tripura (Tripurantaka)

The three demon cities of Tripura, made of gold, silver, and iron, become invincible and wreak havoc. Shiva, as Tripurantaka, destroys the three cities with a single arrow when they align, restoring peace to the universe.

Shaiva Significance: This story illustrates Shiva's power as the destroyer of evil and the upholder of dharma (cosmic order). It symbolizes the destruction of ignorance, ego, and illusion.

7. Shiva and the Demon Andhaka

Andhaka, born from a drop of sweat from Shiva's brow, becomes a powerful demon. He attempts to abduct Parvati, leading to a fierce battle where Shiva kills Andhaka but later forgives him, transforming him into a devoted follower.

Shaiva Significance: This story teaches about forgiveness, transformation, and the idea that even the darkest of beings can be redeemed through divine grace.

8. Shiva and the Burning of Kama

The god of love, Kama, is sent by the gods to awaken Shiva's desire so he can marry Parvati and produce a son to defeat

Tarakasura. However, Shiva, deep in meditation, burns Kama to ashes with his third eye, although later, he revives him at Parvati's request.

Shaiva Significance: This story highlights the power of austerity and control over desires, key principles in Shaivism. It also shows Shiva's compassion in reviving Kama, emphasizing balance in spiritual life.

9. The Story of Rishi Markandeya

Markandeya, destined to die at sixteen, worships Shiva fervently. When Yama, the god of death, comes to take him, Markandeya clings to a Shiva Linga. Shiva appears and rescues him, granting him immortality.

Shaiva Significance: This story underscores the power of devotion and the protective nature of Shiva, who grants liberation and freedom from the cycle of life and death to his true devotees.

10. The Marriage of Shiva and Parvati

After Sati's death, Shiva retreats into deep meditation. Parvati, an incarnation of Sati, performs severe penance to win Shiva's heart. Eventually, Shiva accepts her, and they marry, symbolizing the union of consciousness and energy.

Shaiva Significance: This story represents the union of the divine masculine and feminine, central to Shaivism, emphasizing the balance of energies within and the importance of devotion and perseverance in spiritual practice.

These stories from the Shiv Puran are more than just mythological tales; they are rich with symbolism, spiritual lessons, and the essence of Shaivism. Each story connects deeply with the teachings of Shaivism, guiding devotees on their spiritual journey, offering wisdom, and helping them to understand the divine nature of Shiva. By reflecting on these stories, devotees can draw inspiration and insight to navigate their own lives with greater spiritual awareness and connection to the divine.

Chapter 17

Community and Support

Embarking on a spiritual journey can be profound and transformative, but it's also crucial to find support and connection along the way. This chapter explores the importance of community, resources, and mentorship in your practice of Shaivism.

1. Finding a community

The Importance of Connecting with Others

Connecting with others who are on a similar spiritual path provides valuable support and encouragement. Sharing experiences, challenges, and insights with like-minded individuals can deepen your understanding and enrich your practice.

Sense of Belonging: Being part of a spiritual community helps you feel connected and supported. It offers a sense of belonging and fosters an environment where you can grow together with others who share your values and aspirations.

Learning and Growth: Interacting with a community exposes you to diverse perspectives and teachings. You can learn from others' experiences and gain new insights that enhance your own spiritual journey.

How to Find Local or Online Shaivism Groups?

Local Temples and Centers: Look for local Hindu temples or spiritual centers that offer Shaivism-related activities, classes, or groups. These places often host regular gatherings, study groups, and workshops.

Online Communities: Many online platforms host Shaivism communities where you can join discussions, participate in virtual meetings, and access resources. Websites like Facebook, Reddit, and specialized forums can be valuable for connecting with others.

Spiritual Organizations: Explore organizations dedicated to Shaivism or Hindu spirituality. They may offer online forums, newsletters, and events that can help you find and engage with a community.

Books: Look for books that provide comprehensive insights into Shaivism, its philosophy, and practices. Recommended titles include "The Shiva Sutras" and "Shiva: The Path of the Yogin." These texts offer foundational knowledge and deeper content insights into the teachings of Shaivism.

Websites: Visit websites dedicated to Shaivism and Hindu spirituality. These sites often provide articles, teachings, and resources. Examples include the websites of spiritual organizations and online libraries.

Other Resources: Consider exploring audio recordings, videos, and online courses that offer teachings on Shaivism. These resources can supplement your learning and provide different perspectives on the practice.

Tips for Finding Credible and Helpful Materials

Research and Reviews: Before choosing resources, read reviews and check the credibility of the authors or organizations. Look for materials that are well-regarded by experienced practitioners.

Recommendations: Seek recommendations from trusted members of the Shaivism community or mentors. They can suggest valuable resources based on their own experiences.

Evaluate Content: Ensure that the materials align with the core principles of Shaivism and offer practical insights for your practice. Avoid resources that seem commercial or lack authenticity.

Personal Guidance: A teacher or guru can provide personalized guidance, answer questions, and help you navigate your spiritual journey. Their experience and wisdom are invaluable in understanding and practicing Shaivism.

Support and Encouragement: Mentors offer emotional and spiritual support, helping you overcome obstacles and stay motivated. They can also provide feedback and encouragement as you progress in your practice.

Deepening Understanding: A mentor helps deepen your understanding of the teachings and practices. They can offer insights that are not easily found in books or online resources.

How to Seek Guidance and Support

Finding a Mentor: Look for teachers or mentors through local spiritual centers, online communities, or recommendations from trusted practitioners. Seek someone whose teachings resonate with you and who has a genuine commitment to Shaivism.

Building a Relationship: Establish a respectful and open relationship with your mentor. Be honest about your goals, challenges, and questions. Regular communication and a willingness to learn will help you benefit from their guidance.

Participating in Workshops: Attend workshops, retreats, or seminars led by experienced practitioners. These events provide opportunities to learn directly from teachers and connect with others in the community.

Chapter 18

Embracing the Journey of Self-Transformation

Self-transformation is a profound and ongoing journey. As you continue on your path in Shaivism, it is essential to embrace and navigate the transformative aspects of your spiritual growth. This chapter will guide you through understanding self-transformation, accepting change, and developing resilience.

The Nature and Purpose of Personal Change

Self-transformation is about evolving your inner self. It involves moving beyond old habits, limiting beliefs, and patterns that no longer serve your highest good. This process helps you align more closely with your true nature and the divine essence within you.

Change in your spiritual journey is purposeful. It often leads to greater self-awareness, a deeper connection with the divine, and a more fulfilling life. Embracing this change allows you to grow spiritually and live-in harmony with the principles of Shaivism.

Recognizing Transformation

Signs of Change: You may notice various signs of transformation, such as shifts in your thoughts, emotions, and behaviors. Increased clarity, a sense of inner peace, and a growing understanding of your spiritual path are positive indicators of progress.

Accepting Growth: Understand that transformation is a natural part of your journey. Embrace these changes as opportunities for growth and learning, rather than as obstacles.

Facing Challenges: Change often brings challenges. These may include facing fears, letting go of old patterns, or encountering resistance. Acknowledge these challenges as part of your growth process and approach them with an open mind.

Adapting to Change: Learn to adapt to changes gracefully. Flexibility and openness allow you to navigate challenges with ease and maintain your spiritual focus.

Finding Support

Cultivating Resilience: Resilience is the ability to bounce back from challenges and maintain your spiritual path. Develop resilience by practicing self-care, staying committed to your practices, and cultivating a positive mindset.

Maintaining Faith: Trust in the process of transformation and have faith in your spiritual journey. Remember that each challenge is an opportunity for growth and deeper connection with the divine.

Practical Tips

Mindfulness: Practice mindfulness to stay present and grounded. This helps you manage stress and navigate changes with a calm and centered approach.

Reflection: Reflect regularly on your experiences and progress. Journaling or meditation can provide insights and reinforce your commitment to your path.

Glossary

- **Atman:** The true self or soul in Shaivism, considered to be divine and eternal. It represents the ultimate reality and consciousness within every individual.

- **Bhakti:** Devotion or love for the divine, especially as practiced in various forms of worship and prayer in Shaivism. It is considered a pathway to spiritual growth and connection with Shiva.

- **Kashmir Shaivism:** A school of Shaivism that originated in Kashmir, focusing on the philosophy and practices that emphasize the nature of consciousness and the divine as all-encompassing.

- **Mantra:** Sacred syllables or phrases repeated during meditation or rituals, believed to have spiritual power and the ability to invoke divine energies.

- **Puja:** A ritualistic worship or offering to a deity, involving prayers, offerings, and ceremonies performed to honor and connect with the divine.

- **Sadhana:** Spiritual practice or discipline undertaken to achieve spiritual goals. It includes various forms of meditation, prayer, and ritualistic practices.

- **Shiva:** The principal deity in Shaivism, known as the destroyer and transformer of the universe. Shiva represents the divine consciousness that transcends creation and destruction.

- **Shaivism:** A major tradition within Hinduism that worships Shiva as the supreme deity. It includes a wide range of philosophies and practices focused on achieving union with the divine.

- **Sutras:** Concise, authoritative texts or aphorisms in Hinduism that summarize and encapsulate important teachings. The Shiva Sutras are a key text in Kashmir Shaivism.

- **Tantra:** A set of spiritual practices and philosophical teachings that involve rituals, meditation, and the use of mantras to achieve spiritual realization and transformation.

- **Yajna:** A Vedic ritual of offerings accompanied by chants and prayers, intended to appease and honor the gods. It plays a significant role in ancient Vedic traditions and some Shaiva practices.

- **Yogi/Yogini:** A practitioner of yoga or spiritual disciplines, often dedicated to achieving higher states of consciousness and union with the divine.

- **Vedanta:** A school of Hindu philosophy that focuses on the study and interpretation of the Vedas, particularly concerning the nature of reality and the self.

- **Vedic Studies:** The study of ancient Indian scriptures, including the Vedas, which are foundational texts for understanding the spiritual and ritualistic aspects of Hinduism.

- **Visualization:** A meditation technique involving mental imagery to focus on a specific goal, deity, or aspect of spiritual practice, often used to enhance meditation and personal growth.

- **Self-Realization:** The process of understanding and experiencing one's true self or divine nature, which is a central goal in many spiritual practices, including Shaivism.

- **Sankalpa:** A resolved intention or vow made during spiritual practice, often related to setting a goal or dedicating oneself to a specific spiritual aspiration.

- **Mindfulness:** The practice of maintaining awareness and presence in the moment, which helps in fostering a deeper connection with one's spiritual practice and daily activities.

- **Sacred Space:** A designated area for spiritual practice and meditation, created to foster a serene and focused environment for connecting with the divine and oneself.

Resources and References

This book draws upon a variety of sources to provide a comprehensive introduction to Shaivism and its practices. The information presented is compiled from established texts, teachings, and reputable resources in the field of spiritual studies. Below is a list of the primary sources used in compiling this book:

Books

- *"The Shiva Sutras: The Yoga of Supreme Consciousness"* by Swami Lakshmanjoo

  A fundamental text in Shaivism, offering deep insights into the nature of consciousness and spiritual realization.

- *"The Essence of Shaivism: Teachings from the Kashmir Shaiva Tradition"* by Swami Venkatesananda

  Provides an accessible overview of the teachings of Kashmir Shaivism, elucidating key principles and practices.

- *"Meditations on the Siva Sutras"* by Swami Muktananda

  A guide to understanding and meditating on the Siva Sutras, exploring their significance and application in daily life.

* *"The Complete Works of Swami Sivananda"* by Swami Sivananda

  A comprehensive collection of teachings from one of the most renowned modern Hindu sages, offering insights into various aspects of spiritual practice.

* *"Kashmir Shaivism: The Secret Supreme"* by Swami Lakshmanjoo

  An in-depth study of the philosophy and practices of Kashmir Shaivism, presented by a leading authority on the subject.

Websites

* **Kashmir Shaivism Foundation**

  Provides resources, teachings, and information about the practice and philosophy of Kashmir Shaivism.

* **Shiva Sutras**

  A comprehensive resource on the Siva Sutras, including translations, commentaries, and practical guidance.

* **Sivananda Yoga Vedanta Center**

  Offers teachings and resources related to the practices of Swami Sivananda, including yoga and meditation techniques.

* **Sri Sri Ravi Shankar's Art of Living**

  Features information on meditation, spirituality, and personal development from the perspective of modern spiritual teachings.

Online Courses and Lectures

- **Introduction to Shaivism on Coursera**

  Offers online courses on Shaivism and related spiritual practices, providing a structured approach to learning.

- **Yoga and Meditation Workshops at Yoga Journal**

  Provides workshops and articles on yoga and meditation practices, including those relevant to Shaivism.

- **Online Lectures by Swami Sivananda**

  Features lectures and teachings by Swami Sivananda, covering a range of spiritual topics and practices.

Additional Resources

Meditation Apps:

- **Insight Timer:** Guided meditations and talks on spiritual practices.

- **Headspace:** Meditation sessions and mindfulness exercises.

- **Calm:** Guided meditations and relaxation techniques.

Rituals and Practices:

- Daily Puja (Prayer) Guides and Mantra Practice Instructions for incorporating rituals into daily life.

Acknowledgments

The information presented in this book is derived from a careful study of traditional texts and teachings as well as contemporary resources that provide a modern perspective on Shaivism. I express my gratitude to the authors, scholars, and practitioners whose work has enriched this exploration of Shaivism and made it accessible for readers seeking to deepen their spiritual practice.

Please note that while every effort has been made to accurately represent the teachings and practices of Shaivism, interpretations may vary, and readers are encouraged to explore these resources further for a more comprehensive understanding.